Anonymous

**The Bonn Conferences:**

Impressions Produced by Their Transactions

Anonymous

**The Bonn Conferences:**
*Impressions Produced by Their Transactions*

ISBN/EAN: 9783337773298

Printed in Europe, USA, Canada, Australia, Japan

Cover: Foto ©ninafisch / pixelio.de

More available books at **www.hansebooks.com**

THE

# BONN CONFERENCES.

*IMPRESSIONS PRODUCED BY THEIR*

*TRANSACTIONS.*

BY THE

REV. J. J. OVERBECK, D.D.

LONDON:

TRÜBNER & CO., LUDGATE HILL.

1875.

# THE BONN CONFERENCES.

## IMPRESSIONS PRODUCED BY THEIR TRANSACTIONS.

"The truest expedient is to answer right out when you are asked; the best prudence is not to be a coward; the most damaging folly is to be found out shuffling; and the first of virtues is to tell the truth and shame the devil."—
JOHN HENRY NEWMAN, D.D.

It is a grand sight to see a septuagenarian inaugurate the prodigious work of international Church Union. It was he alone who not only took the initiative, but proceeds single-handed, pointing out the subjects to be treated, the course to be followed, the resolutions to be carried. Indeed, such a master spirit, such vital energy in an aged man, commands the sympathy and admiration of any spectator, whatever his views on the matter may be. Of course, the Romans are not slow in attributing Dr Döllinger's wonderful vitality, zeal, and energy in carrying on his work of Church Union to a feeling of wounded pride, and to a desire of taking revenge on the Ultramontane Church which so shamefully treated him. We cannot be astonished that they think it a spiteful move, when Dr Döllinger teaches the Anglicans how to encounter the Romans disputing the validity of their orders. They compare the author of the "History of the Reformation," who dealt out such heavy blows to the Protestants, with the author of the "Lectures on Church Union," idolised by the very same Protestants. They refer to the author of "The Church and the Churches," who drew

A

the most frightful picture of the Russian Church, and is now not only on speaking terms, but most friendly disposed towards the same. We, on the contrary, cannot but see the victory of a manly spirit over the prejudices of his past life, when he considered the Roman Church the true exponent of all the Catholic truth and the divinely-appointed guardian of Christ's vineyard, when " Roman " and " Catholic " were still convertible terms to him. A man need never be ashamed of giving up wrong notions, which hitherto he thought to be true. Thus Döllinger's present views of Church History and Catholic Doctrine, though very different from what they were before, and though by no means correct and orthodox, do not lower his reputation, but rather increase it, showing that he is a man accessible to reasons, capable of progress, pursuing his object with an untrammelled mind, while the Ultramontanes, stationary and resting on the downy pillow of infallible self-sufficiency, do not feel the slightest want of reconsidering their *status quo*, of sifting their historical sources, of sincerely and thoroughly investigating the traditional proofs of the Catholic dogmas.

But brilliant as may be the obverse of the coin, it has also its reverse. First and foremost, the movement is strictly personal and individual. A man, however great his talents, however comprehensive his mind, is one-sided, he has his peculiar tastes, his likes and dislikes, his hobbies, his pre-conceived notions. Even universal geniuses, like Bacon, Newton, Leibnitz, were not free from these imperfections of human nature. Döllinger is, indeed, one of the greatest Church historians of our age, but he does not pretend to a similar rank in dogmatic theology. Yet this year's subject for discussion was pre-eminently dogmatic. If the late author of the " Symbolik," J. A. Möhler, had lived to see our day, he would, no doubt, have left heretic Rome, and with Döllinger headed the Old Catholic movement. If the great dogmatic theologian, Professor Kuhn, of Tübingen (whose course of lectures Professor Ossinin followed), had summoned up enough courage to resist Rome's temptation, the great Union movement might have been conducted by a

triumvirate of divines, whose varied talents would have made
up each other's deficiencies; whose combined counsels would
have been more apt to concert a sound plan of action, and to
mature it before the subjects were brought forward for discussion ; whose mutual restraining influence would have checked
any unwarranted individual predilection, and borne down
any partiality. Moreover, such a triumvirate would have
saved us the harassing prospect of once losing the one man
who not only was the soul of our Union movement, but the
sole manager, who had assistants indeed, but no partners in
the business. He has his way all alone to himself, and
nobody has to interfere in his proceedings. When he dies,
his personal Union movement is dead too. Another may
take it up, but he is not his natural successor, to whom the
work would devolve by rights. A new work would have to
be founded, for which, of course, the results of Döllinger's
labours might be utilised as stones for the new building, but
certainly on another plan. What is Döllinger's plan in the
selection of subjects to be discussed? I do not know.
Hitherto I could not discover a certain systematic order of
succession in the subjects treated. It appeared to me that
the subjects marked out were taken at random, as it were,
from the periphery of the dogmatic circle, while the central
and fundamental dogmas were left untouched. Yet what
would be the use of agreeing in many separate dogmas, if the
central dogma of " *the Catholic Church and its authority* " is not
agreed upon, is not uniformly understood, believed, and taught?
All believing Christians consider themselves members of the
Catholic Church, but to the Roman Catholics is the Catholic
Church something very different from what it is to the Old
Catholics, and to both, I fear, it is not the same as what it is
to the Orthodox. The Anglicans, as the Protestants generally, are more elastic in their view of the Catholic Church.
Of course a discussion about the Church, its correct notion
and limitation, would have been a gigantic work, would have
roused the spirits to a desperate fight, would have seemed to
deepen the gulf between the different Christian denominations,
to provoke rather the animosities than appease them. No
victory without fight, and no fight undertaken in a Christ-

loving and man-loving spirit for the sake of truth, is without victory. He who fights for the sake of fighting is no more a disciple of Christ than he who says, Peace, where there is no peace. This latter danger is particularly great in ironical transactions. The Tractarians tried to show the harmony of the Thirty-nine Articles and the Council of Trent. Another Anglican (the present Roman Catholic William Palmer?) tried to show the "harmony of Anglican doctrine with the doctrine of the Catholic and Apostolic Church of the East" (Aberdeen, 1846). If a straightforward, outspoken, and unmistakable exposition of the truth wounds and stuns for a moment, it is better, to be sure, than a compromise palliating and obscuring the truth. Even as an intermediate stage, as a stepping-stone to a successive clearer understanding, such compromise is worth less than nothing. If a union is only to be attained by the clever feat of showing that, after all, the different Churches believe the same, that they need not give up any dogma as heretical, since it merely depends on how you explain the words, in order to arrive at an Orthodox meaning ;—if a union of Churches is only to be attained by slowly and imperceptibly infusing a Catholic and Orthodox spirit into them, whilst the heretic poison is rather diluted than secreted—I for one call this flattering and cheating men into the Orthodox Catholic Church, not, however, convincing and converting them. Such, *e.g.*, is the mode of High Church proceeding called "unprotestantising," or more euphemistically, "raising the standard of the Church." It is not the question, whether a certain formula *admits* of an Orthodox interpretation, but whether it can *only* be understood in an Orthodox sense, or might as well conceal a heterodox meaning. We have to ask, Would a man, who holds such or such a dogma, ever have expressed the same in such terms as the disputed formula offers? I allude here particularly to the process of transformation going on in a portion of the English Church since the time of the Tractarians. These Anglo-Catholic Reformers began by laying down, as an indisputable and self-evident axiom, that the Anglican Church was a true and living branch of the Catholic Church. On this supposition they worked on, interpreting and explaining the received Church formularies according to the results of their study of antiquity, although it can be historically proved that the Protestant English Reformers who framed those formularies, understood the words in a genuine Protestant sense. Such a non-natural twisting of words could not fail to open the eyes of many of the leading men, of a Newman, Wilberforce, Manning, Palmer, &c., to the truth that their Church had fallen into schism and heresy, and thereby forfeited its claim to Catholicity. Even Allies, who had written a voluminous and very instructive book to clear the English Church from the charge of schism, found his arguments untenable, and joined Rome. It is wonderful how these Anglo-Catholics, among whom there are many first-rate scholars of Catholic antiquity, shut their eyes to the glaring fact, imprinted on almost every page of the history of Undivided Christendom, that, as soon as a heresy turned up in the Church, the heretical party was cut off from the Church, and thus the poison secreted from the body of the Church. The Donatists, who were much nearer the Catholic truth than the Anglicans, were no Catholics. What was the use of their teaching almost the whole Catholic truth? They were no Catholics. If thus the Anglicans go on unprotestantising and catholicising their Church more and more, it is, no doubt, a good and acceptable work, preparing the way which leads to the true Catholic Church, but as yet they are without the pale of the Catholic Church. A Church, which is not Catholic, cannot change itself by self-improvement into a Catholic Church, but must come out and join the Catholic Church. This is the principal fault that lies at the root of the Anglo-Catholic Reform movement in the English Church, viz., the entirely wrong notion of the Catholic Church. From this wrong notion follows the extraordinary idea that the Catholic Church consists of three branches: the Roman, Greek, and Anglican Churches, though the first and second consider each other schismatic and heretic, and both have no communion with the third. If such be the Church with which the Holy Ghost has promised to abide, leading her into *all* truth, common sense will scarcely be able to solve the riddle: where and what is then the truth, since the three branches or component parts of the Catholic Church contradict each other? Or shall we perhaps wait till science and research have smoothed the way, and brought the conflicting parties into harmony? But where is then, *at present*, the Catholic Church leading us into all truth, our infallible guide, presided over by the Holy Ghost? This Church is not an historical and antiquarian puzzle still to be found out. She must *exist*, not in an airy, ideal, and intangible form, we must be able to grasp her, to lay our hands on her. She must be the city on the top of the mountain, visible to every eye that will see.

From the wrong notion of the Church follows also the grave mistake that only *Corporate Reunion* is desirable, but *Individual Secession* objectionable. As no Catholic can advise a Christian to remain outside the Catholic Church till all his co-religionists are pleased to follow him inside, it is plain that any one advocating this principle must recognise the English Church as a fully Catholic Church.

Now my readers will say, What has this exposé of Anglican shortcomings to do with the Bonn Conference? Is it not simply an undue digression from the main subject? My readers shall presently see that every word is to the purpose, and that Döllinger, to a great extent, stands on Anglican ground. Döllinger advocates " Corporate Reunion," which implies, as we saw before, the supposition that the English Church is a true and living branch of the Catholic Church. Now the English Church teaches heresies, or (if any one might cleverly interpret them away) at least permits authoritatively to teach heresies. It is true, heresy might *clandestinely* be disseminated even in the Catholic Church, but as soon as discovered it is exploded. In the English Church the minister may teach and preach the Zwinglian doctrine of the Lord's Supper without let or hindrance (and it is taught by the vast majority of ministers). He may inveigh against Sacerdotalism and Sacramentalism, and warn from such doctrines as importations from Rome. Neither Bishop nor people object to it. Döllinger knows this state of things, or can be expected to know it. Consequently, he admits of a Catholic Church teaching heresy, or at least permitting heresy to be taught publicly and authoritatively from the pulpit, in pastoral letters, in official accounts. *We Orthodox proclaim, as first and fundamental principle of the one true Church of Christ, that it must contain all Catholic dogmas, pure and unaltered, nothing more and nothing less.* He who adds to or subtracts from this revealed truth, is no more member of the one Orthodox Catholic Church which Christ and His Apostles founded. This Church admits not of the slightest admixtion of heresy, not of any dogmatic compromise, not of any latitudinarian or elastic interpretation. Our Church knows not of an amalgamation of truth and error, light and darkness, Orthodoxy and Heterodoxy. Therefore Romans and Protestants call our faith *petrified* or *crystallised,* because it is sealed up in the *Seven Œcumenic Synods,* and is not handed out for the free handling of *dogmatic development.* Or shall we perhaps call the English Church *semi-Catholic,* as we speak of semi-Arians and semi-Pelagians? Also this subterfuge is of no avail. In the domain of truth there is no twilight, no middle term of half-truth. One is either a full Catholic, or no Catholic at all. Döllinger's Anglican idea of the Catholic Church may, indeed, have originated from the sad and anomalous position of the Old Catholics generally opposite the Roman Church, which they declare to be heretical, and still they partook of its sacraments, and wished to continue its intercommunion, had not the Romans (more consistent from their point of view) broken such an unnatural bond. As, particularly in the mind of an Orthodox Christian, Heterodoxy must be excluded from the true Catholic Church, every sound Catholic feels that a Church cannot pretend to Catholicity, in which a party, holding all or almost all Catholic truth, continues living side by side with two other parties professedly Protestant, one boasting of their legitimate Protestant forefathers Luther, Calvin, Cranmer, Jewell, &c., the other claiming the same Protestant descent, but glorying in having carried out the Protestant principle to its lawful conclusion, *i.e.,* Rationalism. This tripartite division of the English Church is a patent fact, and Döllinger could not and did not ignore it. But he calls these divisions the three " *schools of thought,*" which expression is apt to misrepresent the thing and mislead the auditory. The Catholic Church, too, had always different "schools of thought." There was the school of Antioch opposed to that of Alexandria. There was in our times a Liberal school (Jahn, Hug, Hirscher, Hortig, &c.) opposed to the Ultramontane school. There was in the Russian Church the Conservative school represented by Yavorsky, and the Liberal school represented by Procopovitch. But now mark the signal difference between these Catholic "schools of thought" and those Protestant and Anglican. The Catholics, to whichever "school of thought" they belonged, held *all* the dogmas of their Church, and differed only on the points not contained in the revealed truth, and left to their free research and discussion. If such a "school of thought" overstepped its limits, and trespassed on the ground of revealed truth, it was censured and discontinued, or, in case of resistance, it was cut off from the Church, and its votaries formed an heretical body. The harmless designation "school of thought" was no more applied to them, but they were simply called heretics. On this ground we find the application of "schools of thought" to the three parties in the English Church, not only wrong, but downright misrepresenting and misleading.

This consideration leads us to another question : Which is the position the Anglicans take in the Bonn Conference? Are there two contracting parties, or three? Are the Anglicans admitted on equal terms with the Orthodox, *i.e.*, as Catholics? Or do they range with the rest of the Protestants? Is our Church Union not to be effected till the Anglicans are ready to join? Is no resolution to be carried, save with the consent and agreement of the Anglicans? If these questions are answered in favour of the Anglicans, the Döllinger Union movement will prove A TOTAL FAILURE, and must prove so, because it would not have a sound Catholic ground. Döllinger's first invitation to the Conference was most acceptable to all who wished for a Union of the different Christian Churches on a truly Orthodox basis, for this invitation declared the dogmas of the Church of Undivided Christendom, *i.e.*, of the Catholic Church before the Great Schism rent East and West asunder, to be the basis and standard of the Conference. This would bring us down to the ninth century, even if we date the Schism as early as possible. At all events, the Seven Œcumenical Synods, on which the Orthodox. Church rests, belong to the Church of Undivided Christendom. Accordingly, we expected nobody to take part in the transactions of the Conference, who did not accept the Seven Œcumenical Synods, and all the dogmas proclaimed by the same. We were greatly astonished to see the Anglicans admitted not as spectators, but as partakers, since they do not accept the Seven Œcumenical Synods, and consequently do not stand on the basis laid down in the invitation. We were still more astonished to read in the report of the first Conference held in 1874 (Bericht, p. 78), Döllinger: " In the invitation to this ·Conference, the doctrine of the Undivided Church has been designated as the basis of the transactions. *This is thus the same basis which also Meyrick has proposed.*"

I scarcely believed my own eyes, as I had just in the lines immediately preceding the above quotation read Hogg's explanation of Meyrick's proposal. This proposal (he says)· " is to that effect, that the Conference might *confine itself to establish the doctrine of the first five or six centuries.*"

Thus Meyrick's basis is *not* the same basis as that of Döllinger's invitation. Yet Döllinger says it is. How can we explain this apparent contradiction? Or how can Döllinger escape this dilemma? He knows Church history too well to be aware that Undivided Christendom does not extend to the fifth or sixth century, but to the ninth. Thus Döllinger does not redeem his pledge, and shifts his ground, or he calls Undivided Christendom only that portion of Undivided Christendom which. Anglicans are pleased to admit. But such a conception would, at least, require an explanatory clause in the invitation. However, also this year's invitation simply refers to the Undivided Church. Did ever the Undivided Church doubt the Seven Sacraments? Why then were they brought into discussion? Evidently for no other reason than to settle the Anglican controversy. In this way we lose our ground, our *unconquerable ground* of Undivided Christendom, and drift away from our Catholic

moorings into the open sea of Protestant deformation.
Archpriest Yanysheff very clearly and appropriately pointed
out (Bericht, 1874, p. 25) how easy our task would be,
if we seriously and *with full earnest* stuck to the ground of
the Undivided Church, to its Seven Œcumenical Synods and
Seven Sacraments. Alas! how far we are from this pious
wish we saw this year, when at my merely mentioning the
Seven Œcumenical Synods, a storm of indignation arose,
which must clearly have proved to my Orthodox brethren
that *our basis is not the Church of Undivided Christendom,
but that we are far, far away from it, on a roaring sea, and no
land in sight.*

Let no man think that I am an enemy of Anglicans, and
therefore try to keep them back from our Union movement.
I have many friends among them, both laymen and clergymen, and we both exchange our views frankly and openly
without the slightest abatement of our mutual friendly feel-
ings. But what I thoroughly disapprove is that Anglicans,
who *do not and cannot accept the basis* of the Bonn Conference,
enter into the business as if it was a matter of course, and
are admitted without the slightest reluctance. Thus the only
safe principle of Union is sacrificed to Anglican propensities.
But had then the Anglicans, who came, to be sent away or
only to be admitted as spectators? Neither of the two.
Courtesy bids us to be polite, justice to acknowledge their
good-will, and our own interest to keep hold of them, leading
them by further instruction to the faith of Undivided Christendom. Why should not sittings of Anglicans *on their own
basis* be arranged, in which Old Catholics and Orthodox
might take part, while the proper sittings of the Conference
*on the basis of Undivided Christendom* would only comprise
Old Catholics and Orthodox as real members and voters?
The Anglicans might attend our sittings, and see how far
their own standard of belief allows them to meet us. *Our
resolutions, however, must be entirely free from Anglican
interference, entirely independent of Anglican consent.* Then
only our progress will be steady and rapid. Then only we
are spared a great deal of superfluous controversy, which
now is thrown into our way, and remarkably hinders our

progress. Why should we, to please a third party, clear away all the rubbish which the Reformation has heaped up in every department of theology, and obstruct our own way in order not to get so quickly to our end? Would this not seem unwise and irrational? The sooner we (Orthodox and Old Catholics) are ready, *i.e.*, the sooner our Churches are united, the sooner we can with combined forces throw our heart and soul into the work of uniting Anglicans and the other Protestants with our Church. Let them now already, within certain limits, take part in our movement, but let them not arrest, disturb, or even wreck it.

It is strange, and cannot have escaped the notice of an attentive observer, that the German Protestants, who are very friendly disposed towards the Old Catholics, share their churches with them, have daily intercourse with them, and do all that lies in their power to promote their ends—I say it is strange that these German Protestants take no part in the Union movement. I know many Anglicans will confidently answer: "No wonder, Germany is a country of unbelievers, who cannot feel an interest in the Union question." But they do not know that there is still a goodly number of German Protestants who do believe as much as Dean Howson and other Anglican members of the Conference. Why do they keep back? Our answer is: "Because they feel they cannot honestly and conscientiously accept the basis laid down by Döllinger." Truth and modesty forbid them to intrude and encroach on a field of action to which they are not invited. The English are different. Their national character has been trained and fashioned by their history, and history has imprinted on this character a feeling of superiority. The Englishman feels himself master of the world, and acts accordingly; and he thinks it quite natural that other people should share his self-estimation. No work is too heavy, no undertaking too difficult and expensive, for he devotes all his energies to his task, and has plenty of money to pay. Therefore he is determined to have his say and to be heard. This feature of character makes many an Englishman haughty and overbearing. The Old Catholics will, no doubt,

remember, how Bishop Wordsworth made his appearance at
the Cologne Congress, distributed pamphlets without asking
leave from the Old Catholics, and made himself quite at
home, as if he was in his diocese. A prominent Old
Catholic said to me : "That gentleman seems to have quite
forgotten that he is only our guest, for he fancies himself
the master of the house." This particular lineament of
English character may prove injurious or even fatal to our
movement. For if the Anglicans are bent on having it all
to themselves, if they strive to have the casting vote, if they
succeed in dragging the Old Catholics along with them,
whither the Orthodox cannot follow—the end of it would
be one more branch of the English Church. Such a termina-
tion of our Union movement would be deplorable, for more
than one reason, chiefly because it would make a large breach
in the wall of Old Catholicism, through which Anglican
Protestantism would break in and sap the Catholic foundations. Some signs are pointing in that direction, and in
some doctrines the Old Catholics have already further withdrawn from Rome, and drawn nearer to the Anglicans than
the Orthodox.

But let us not give way to apprehensions, nor conjure up
dark visions. Let us consider them passing clouds vanish-
ing from before the rising sun. Still it is never in vain to
look out in every direction, and closely follow the course the
movement takes. Never mind, let the Anglicans have a
deliberative voice in the discussions, but never a decisive
voice or casting vote. Moreover, it would be a change for
the better, if Döllinger could make up his mind not to speak
of the English Church as a Unit, since it is a motley Aggre-
gate of the most different persuasions, and address himself
exclusively to the so-called Anglo-Catholics within the
Establishment.

Now let us muster the principal results of the Conferences,
test them on their merits, and examine whether any of the
achievements have been attended by practical consequences.

The first seven theses (Bericht, 1874, p. 15–17) are mere
statements of doctrines held by the Old Catholics, Orthodox,
Anglicans, and (with the exception of the first and seventh)

even by liberal Roman Catholics. The momentous eighth Proposition runs as follows :—" We acknowledge that the number of Sacraments was fixed at seven first in the twelfth century, and then was received into the general teaching of the Church, *not as a tradition coming down from the Apostles* or from the earliest times, *but as the result of theological speculation.*" We read this heterodox thesis in blank astonishment, and doubt very much if many even among the Old Catholics will submit to Döllinger's verdict, since all of them were taught to consider the Septenary Number of Sacraments as a dogma. Apparently this proposition has been framed to make an approach to the Anglicans, who teach in their official Catechism only two sacraments, and admit some of the others only as a sort of secondary sacraments. If the Septenary Number was *not a tradition coming down from the Apostles, but the result of theological speculation,* the Septenary Number MAY NOT be taught as a Dogma (cf. Bericht, 1875, p. 8, No. 4, C.) ; and if Döllinger would not be willing to withdraw this proposition, all hope of re-union would now already be gone. Yanysheff declared in the name of the Orthodox that he must *insist upon* the recognition of the Seven Sacraments (as Dogma). Though " as Dogma " is not added in Yanysheff's reply, the context (page 25) shows that it is meant so. It is thus unpardonable that Meyrick, in his Address, delivered in Lincoln Cathedral, August 29th 1875, coolly says : " At the first (Bonn) Conference, incredible as it appeared beforehand, *an agreement* was come to by Old Catholics, members of the Oriental Church and English Churchmen on (8th) the Septenary Number of Sacraments." We wonder why Döllinger did not find the traditional proofs, displayed in every Orthodox and Roman Catholic Dogmatic Theology for every single Sacrament, sufficient to establish the Septenary Number of Sacraments. Or did he find any other rite or ceremony endowed with a power working " *ex opere operato?* " Yet this he would have been obliged to show. It is not the name by which the Septenary Number of Sacraments was to be defined, but their operation. Ritter in his " Handbuch der Kirchengeschichte," vol. ii. page 81, says : " At last it must be still remarked, that by some modern scholars of the Evangelical Church the reception and teaching of *Seven Sacraments* has been ascribed to this age, particularly to the twelfth century. . Let us here only remark that the Greek Church, though censuring just at this period everything in which the Latins differed from her, never reproach them the number of Sacraments, but professes likewise Seven Sacraments, as the Ritual Books, edited by Goar and Arkudius, the Confession of Faith of Michael Paläologus, and the censure of the Augsburg Confession on the part of the Constantinopolitan Patriarch, Jeremias, show." And it was just the Septenary Number of Sacraments which was most deeply impressed on the conviction of Christians. Thus, the Nestorians and Monophysites teach Seven Sacraments, although they do not agree which they are (cf. " The Nestorians and their Rituals," by Badger, vol ii., page 404; and " The Syrian Churches," by J. W. Etheridge, pages 59 and 144). Or shall we suppose that the Nestorians and Monophysites borrowed their Catechism from their Orthodox and Roman Catholic enemies? Let us conclude with a passage from Archbishop Macarius's " Théologie Dogmatique Orthodoxe," tom. ii., p. 374 : " Qaunt au nombre des sacrements, le protestantisme ne s'est pas borné à rabaisser la véritable idée de la substance et de l'efficacité des sacrements; il a porté une *sacrilége* main sur leur nombre." I cannot think, and may not think, that many Old Catholics share Döllinger's view about the Seven Sacraments, otherwise our hopes and prospects for a reunion would be very poor. But here the question arises: " Are we transacting with the Old Catholics or simply with Döllinger?" The number of Old Catholics present at both Conferences was very small and very passive. But, perhaps, the Old Catholics consider Döllinger not only as their spokesman but as their trustworthy guide? No, indeed, they do not. Was it not Döllinger who warned them from leaving " the great Catholic Church," from " erecting altar against altar," from forming congregations of their own? Had they followed Döllinger's request, where would Old Catholicism now be? It would be such a pity if Döllinger, in consequence of his predilection for the English Church, would lead the Old Catholics to wrong steps. The Old Catholics are a *reformable* Church, which in a wonderfully short time has done away with almost every Roman error and abuse. Now it stands, as it were, on the threshold of Orthodoxy, ready to revive the true Catholic Church of the West, as it was before the great Schism, and the bond would perhaps already be realised, were it not for the English Church. This Church is *irreformable*, first, because it does not admit that it harbours heresies,* secondly,

---

* That the English Church harbours heresies is a fact acknowledged even by Anglicans, though naturally they are touchy and reserved on this point, because any Church teaching heresies, or tolerating heresies to be taught, has undeniably forfeited its Catholic character. Let us now hear some Anglican voices. EX ORE TUO TE JUDICO ! The *Church News* (now incorporated in the *Church Review*) of September 18, 1867, writes : "A Church of course compromises the truth if it deliberately reckons heretics among its members, but can the same be said of an Establishment ? [Church and Establishment—a distinction without a difference !] Supposing the Catholic faith and that alone to be established in the first place, it becomes manifest that if the authorities of the Church fail in their duties, unbelief and heresy will creep in among its members. It is quite conceivable then that the State may refuse to shut out from such privileges, as membership in the Establishment affords, those who have become what they are by the fault of the Church. The State may think it to be for the good of the nation to expel no one who does not expel himself, and to permit all those to be recognised teachers in the Establishment who do not hold tenets utterly subversive of its existence. At all events this seems to be the condition of things which we are fast approaching ; and if error is not more favoured than truth, and truth is allowed to make such way as it can by its own merits, we shall have to be content. *It is scarcely too much to say that three different religions or forms of Christianity are at present established in England.* Fundamental differences on the Incarnation separate Catholic, Protestant, and Rationalist, and underlie the divergence of the super-structures they build upon this doctrine. . . . Theological ignorance and neglect on the part of the English bishops and clergy have been the cause of *the heresies at present existing in the Establishment,* and it is just that the Church should suffer for her own sins. Those who think the State should interfere and sever from connection with herself those *whom the Church has first allowed to grow up in error,* and then has made no attempt to restrain or correct, should be made to perceive that this would be to hold one body responsible for the faults of another, and that it should undertake all the trouble and loss of correction, while the original offender should escape scot-free. . . Dr Stanley is an officer of the State, so is Dr M'Neile, so is Dr Pusey. The religions they believe have some points in common, and are held in juxta-position by subscription to the same formularies, *which each understand in, or twist into, their own sense.* . . In theory, none will deny that the English Church holds the Creed of Ephesus, Nicæa, and Chalcedon, on the Incarnation, *although practically most of her members are unsound. Almost all the early heresies have risen again* among those who nevertheless repeat the words that condemn them. We cannot as yet escape the taunt *that error is as welcome in the Establishment as truth,* and indeed more so, while the Church, however tacitly condemning error, *is herself too much practically tainted with it,* to drive out the evil." The Rev. A. H. Stanton, a well-known Ritualistic clergyman in London, said at the twelfth anniversary of the English Church Union : " I say at present many of us feel that we are bound to a society by the Church Establishment, *which is divided into three parties,* ALL TEACHING DIFFERENT DOCTRINES, *and the worst of it is, that those doctrines are set before the people of England as the doctrines of the Church of England, and upheld by the Establishment as such.* How can we tell

because it cannot alter anything in doctrine or practice
without the sanction of Parliament. Thus if the Old Catholics
wish for a union with the Anglicans, they must draw near to
them (not *vice-versa*) sacrifice their Catholic ground, and
in the same proportion withdraw from Orthodoxy

Döllinger's effective speech in favour of the Orthodox

people that truth is one and that dogmatic truth is necessary, and at the same
time vote for the continuance of an Establishment which holds together three different parties, *teaching three totally different doctrines?*" A practical proof of
Latitudinarian heresy, showing that the very elements of a Catholic dogmatic
sense are unknown to Anglican clergymen, is the answer which the Rev. R. T.
West returned to Mr Stanton: "There was a point in which Mr Stanton, I thought,
raised a note of discord which was unnecessary, and that is *the great difference of
the doctrines taught by the parties in the Church.* Those differences appear much
more upon the surface than they are at bottom, *and I must say it is not a good
thing to magnify any differences which exist.* So long as the different parties in
the English Church hold the great cardinal doctrines of the Incarnation, the
Atonement, the Resurrection, the Ascension, and the doctrine of the Blessed
Trinity, *we cannot say we differ very much on the doctrines of the Catholic faith.*"
But even "the great cardinal doctrines," which Mr West refers to, are not safe
in the English Church, as we shall hear presently from Dr Pusey, who in an inte-
resting letter to the "Literary Churchman" (cf. "Orth. Cath. Review," vol. i. p. 30,
seq.) writes as follows: "Dissensions within the Church! There are, alas!
no lack of them, nor of such as are of the very gravest character. . . . The
inspiration and truth of Holy Scripture. . . . the inerrancy of the Apostles, nay,
of our Lord himself,—these are among the subjects of ʽdissensions.' Within
the substance of his revelation, the doctrine of the Atonement, the divinity of
our Lord, judgment to come, are among the subjects of ʽdissension.' In regard
to the evidences of the Faith there is ʽdissension,' whether there be either
miracle or prophecy. The Bishop of London [the present Archbishop of Canterbury and Primate of England] in his recent Charge, expressed a *hope* (which in
itself implies a misgiving) that none of the clergy would deny our Lord's Resurrection. It has been contemplated, in quarters in which this is startling enough,
*that the truth of our Lord's Resurrection will have to be left an open question among
ministers of the English Church.* If there be any heresy which does not find
acknowledgment among the members of this school, it is because it contains, not
too much error, but too much truth."

The heretic character of the English Church we see also, indirectly and by
implication, from the judgment Anglicans pass on the Orthodox Church. The
Archbishop of Canterbury (when still Bishop of London) said: "We must ask
calmly, but very seriously, how far these Churches [*i.e.*, the Orthodox and the
Roman] are exerting themselves *to escape from that idolatrous worship of the
Lord's Mother. . . There can be no union on our part which overlooks the deadly
sins of idolatry,*" etc. Dean Close, one of the foremost Evangelicals in the English
Church, wrote in a letter to the *Carlisle Examiner:* "I was praying, and
still pray, that we may never be reduced into *an unnatural union with* ʽ error'—
such a union as has been proposed and vindicated by many Ritualists, a union
with *the Greek Church, which is unsound on the doctrine of the Holy Trinity.*" And
at an Anti-Ritualistic meeting at Carlisle, the same Dean said, that "*the false and
corrupt Greek Church's* . . . worship is debased and degrading, and superstitious
in the extreme. *Sooner be my hand withered than I should hold it out to the
Eastern or Western Churches.*" (Cf. "Orth. Cath. Review," vol. i. pp. 126, 127, 253.)
These are also *Anglican voices,* may they serve as a wholesome supplement and
antidote for those who judge Anglicanism by its representatives at the Bonn
Conferences!

Church, was naturally hailed by the members of this Church, though we could not expect anything else from the master of Dr Plohler, who was the first Roman Catholic scholar who tried to do full justice to the Orthodox. The speaker's enthusiastic words must have transported the listeners; but when the words lie printed before your eyes, you can fix and ponder them. Thus we read, that in the Oriental Churches (of course the speaker can only mean the Orthodox ones) the Apostolic deposit of Doctrine and Sacraments (Heilsmittel) had been "preserved unimpaired and *essentially* unadulterated" (Bericht, 1874, p. 22). Now the Orthodox·Church maintains that her doctrine (*i.e.*, her dogmata), being exactly that of the Church of Undivided Christendom, is "*absolutely* unadulterated," not in consequence of a merely human and historical process, but on the supernatural ground of the divine promise that the Holy Spirit will abide with the Church, and lead her into all truth. *Was this Church of divine promise not the Church of Undivided Christendom?* If not, where was this Church of divine promise? Did it perhaps embrace at the same time the Nestorian, Monophysite, Monothelite, Pelagian, Donatist, and other sectarian Churches? I trust Döllinger will unhesitatingly and unreservedly declare, that this Church of divine promise was, and is, and ever will be, "the Church of Undivided Christendom," *at the exclusion of any other Church, past, present, or future.* Now, when the West separated from this ground, while the East faithfully adhered to it, was "the Church of Undivided Christendom" gone? Or did the deserter not share the same fate that befell the former deserters, the Nestorians, Monophysites, etc.? And when the separated West by continual innovations, hierarchical tyranny, and political dominion succeeded in erecting a worldly edifice, more magnificent and powerful than the Arian Church at St Jerome's time, this Dome burst in thousand splinters at the time of the Reformation. This was naturally the doom and punishment of a Church that had deserted the holy ground, once her own. Does Döllinger perhaps mean that, when the West forsook the Church of Undivided Christendom, the Holy Spirit followed it, or divided His operations between the two rival

B

Churches? And when the West broke again in pieces, had
the Holy Spirit to divide again in as many splinters? No,
let us be true and consistent. Only " the Church of Undivided Christendom " is the Church of divine promise, is
the Church guided by the Holy Spirit into all truth, and no
other Church beside her. And because we know this, and
firmly believe this, *we cannot give up or change a dogma of
our Church of Undivided Christendom, nor can we add any to
the number*, without sinning against the Holy Ghost. It is
not Eastern pride or obstinacy that prompts the Orthodox
to resist any Western flattery or bait, it is simply a deeply-
seated feeling of truth. He admits the Western superiority
in learning, in arts and sciences, and all other worldly accom-
plishments, he lowers himself even more than he needs, but
do not touch his TRUST, the infallible dogmatic deposit in his
Church. Here is no concession, no compromise, no bargain-
ing, no shifting, no colouring. *You must accept all the dogmas as they are*, because they are the truth of the Holy Ghost.
*Only on this plain condition a Reunion is possible.* There is
no other back-door to get in. If once the dogmatic ground
is truly and sincerely accepted, you will be astonished how
liberal the Orthodox are, how far they are from imposing on
you Eastern rites or customs, how willing they are in assist-
ing you to rebuild your National Churches on the common
Orthodox ground.

Thus we must insist on *" absolutely* unadulterated," and
must decline Döllinger's *" essentially."* We do not know
where Döllinger may fix the line of demarcation for the
*essence*. The Orthodox is utterly ignorant of distinguishing
in a dogma a shell and a kernel; to him the whole dogma
is pure essence; he does not envelop the dogma in a cover of
inferior stuff. This is a Protestant invention, sublimating,
refining, and evaporating the truth to such a degree that at
last little is left.

Further on we have to notice (Bericht, 1874, p. 33), a
thesis, not only superfluous, but rather obnoxious, tending
to shift and obscure our debating ground. It is thesis 9 a:
" We agree, that the genuine tradition, *i.e.*, the unbroken
transmission, partly oral, partly in writing, of the doctrine

delivered by Christ and the Apostles, is an authoritative source of teaching for all successive generations of Christians. This tradition is partly to be found *in the consensus of the great ecclesiastical bodies standing in historical continuity with the primitive Church*, partly to be gathered by scientific method from *the written documents of all centuries.*"

The Orthodox would say : "Apostolic traditions are those which are recognised as such by all the members of the Orthodox Church, because this Church is at present the only legitimate representative of the Church of Undivided Christendom." The Orthodox Church cannot recognise any ecclesiastical bodies beside her as existing *de jure* without destroying her own *raison d'être*, *i.e.*, her claim to absolute Orthodoxy. If she allows herself to be made "one of the many," she is irretrievably lost. If she would make the Apostolical traditions dependent on the Consensus of a lot of heterodox bodies (the number of which even Döllinger might be puzzled to specify), their extent might speedily shrink together to an invisible size. Would it not be the height of stupidity, to expect the Orthodox to co-operate in their self-destruction, to reduce their arms, because their adversaries have not as many? We had already one specimen of what the required "Consensus" means, viz., Döllinger's opposition to the recognition of the Apostolic tradition of the Seven Sacraments—and we have enough with this one specimen.

If the Apostolic tradition is partly to be gathered "*from the written documents of all centuries,*" I fear we shall never be able to exhaust it, or adequately to describe it. Such a superhuman task is far beyond the power of realisation. It is quite a different thing, to enjoin it as a duty on a Professor of dogmatic theology, to lay the written documents of all centuries under contribution, in order to substantiate the Apostolic traditions known at all times, and always taught by the Church.

The discussion of this momentous thesis in the Conference was most insignificant; and the Orthodox objections were scarcely taken any notice of. Yet we read on p. 35: "*The thesis is granted.*" Why is non marked, by whom? Certainly not by the Orthodox, who never withdrew their objections.

We are happy to point out the particularly felicitous wording of the 13th thesis: "We acknowledge, that the practice of the commemoration of the faithful departed, *i.e.*, the calling down of a richer outpouring of Christ's grace upon them, has come down to us from the primitive Church, and is to be preserved in the Church."

As the Anglicans and Americans admit that the teaching of their Churches is silent on this point, they (or at least part of them) scrupled to engage themselves. We do not wonder at this result, as the very Primate of the English Church, in his letter to the Patriarch of Constantinople, decidedly declined the acceptance of this doctrine.

The thesis on the Eucharistic Sacrifice (p. 46 seq.) is not directly incorrect, but the beginning words may give rise to a misconception. They run as follows: "The Eucharistic Celebration in the Church is not a continuous repetition or renewal of the *propitiatory sacrifice* offered once for ever by Christ upon the cross," etc. This *seems* to imply, that the Eucharistic Celebration is not a *propitiatory sacrifice*, which would contradict the teaching of the Orthodox Church. St Cyril of Jerusalem calls it expressly θυσία τοῦ ἱλασμοῦ, and the *Confessio Orthodoxa* (quæst. 107) is most explicit on this head. If the word "propitiatory" had been left out, no misunderstanding would have been possible. I wish distinctly to be understood, that I do not suppose Döllinger to deny the propitiatory character of the Mass, but simply that the shifting wording may lead to such a misunderstanding.

The supplement to the *Church Review* (October 10, 1874), remarks on the history of this thesis: "At a private meeting between Dr Döllinger and the leading Anglicans, a *somewhat ambiguous* formula on the Eucharistic Sacrifice and Presence was agreed upon, partly cast in the language of the Epistle to the Hebrews, which was afterwards submitted to the Conference. The Easterns looked askance at it, and took pains, one after another, to lay down the doctrine of their own Church on the subject in very unmistakable terms, borrowed, we presume, from the Orthodox Catechism,

but closely coincident with the language of the Council of
Trent as to the identity of the Sacrifice offered on the Cross
and in the Mass for the sins of the living and the dead.
They said, if that was the meaning of the article, they
would accept it, but not else. Dr Döllinger assured them
that they were right; *but he did not think it necessary to
translate their remarks into English,* and it may be questioned
whether Dean Howson, *e.g.,* who had previously declined to
vote for an article asserting prayer for the dead, would have
been equally ready to accept their interpretation of the
formula. In this, as in other cases—notably in the very
elastic article on the number of the sacraments—we cannot
help thinking *that more success was achieved in hitting on a
vaguely comprehensive form of words than in ascertaining or
securing any real unity of belief."*

I shall have to touch still two questions : the *Anglican
Orders,* and the *Filioque.*

The settlement of the first question is by no means
pressing, for the agreement of the Anglicans and Orthodox
is far from approaching, yet the question would for us be of
any practical significance only on the eve of Reunion. But
for such a Reunion there is at present not the slightest
shade of prospect, yea it is clearly *impossible,* as long as the
English Church is in State bondage. One instance will
show it you *ad oculos.* You are unanimous in condemning
the unlawful interpolation of the *Filioque* into the Niceno-
Constantinopolitan Creed. Well, *can* you strike it out of
the Creed, even if you would ? *No, you cannot!* Your
hands are tied. You have to ask for an Act of Parliament !
Yet the Orthodox never can think of a Union with you,
before this objectionable clause has been removed, officially
and authoritatively. In both the Conferences so much has
been talked about the validity of Anglican Orders, that
some of the Orthodox really thought it would be time that
our Church authorities took the matter into consideration.
But what business have we to settle the difficulties of
heterodox Churches, with which we have no Church connection whatever ? Shall we perhaps not settle at the same
time the validity of Swedish and Moravian orders ? If we

are once meddling in other people's affairs, we might as well do it on a larger scale. My humble opinion is, let us leave this question alone, as we have left it alone these three hundred years. When the Anglicans are at our gate, we will look more closely into the question, for then only it will be a question that concerns us. Here I cannot refrain from correcting Liddon, when he says, the late Metropolitan Philaret of Moscow had only read Roman Catholic authors on the matter. I know from reliable sources, that he also read Stubbs's exposé on the question. He was not baited by the absurd Nag's Head fable, but there were other considerations of a more serious nature. I earnestly warn my Orthodox brethren from prematurely and unnecessarily embarking in this complicated affair of recognising the Anglican Orders. Let me hint here only at two difficulties generally overlooked: 1. The recognition of Anglican Orders *is by no means an exclusively historical question* (as Döllinger thinks), *but it is also an essentially dogmatic question,* as I have shown in my " Reconsideration of Anglican Claims " (" Orthod. Cath. Review " vol. III.) And this dogmatic difficulty is by no means the one to which Döllinger alludes (Bericht, 1875, p. 94), but the Protestant doctrine of the General Priesthood, at all times since the Reformation held by the important Evangelical section of the English Church. And as to the historical side of the question, let us not blindly follow Döllinger's verdict, for, though he may be one of the greatest Church historians of our age, he is at the same time one of the greatest admirers of the Anglican Church, and his partiality compels us to be cautious. 2. This question is a loophole, through which we might easily and insensibly glide into open Protestantism. I will show you how. The American Convention has committed itself to the grave mistake to decide that " *no reason exists to think the Swedish succession lost.*" And in consequence of this decision, *formal acts of intercommunion* took place, when the Bishop of Illinois visited Sweden. Thus a Swedish Priest might minister in the American Church and become Bishop. Would this not vitiate the Anglican Succession, even if it were unexceptionably sound? Also

Anglican Bishops recognised the Swedish Orders. Thus Dr Gray, Metropolitan of South Africa, *formally notified to the Archbishop of Upsala*, as to other Prelates, the excommunication of Dr Colenso. So you get into a fair way of letting in undoubtedly Lutheran blood into the Anglican system. In England the question has, indeed, not yet been settled, Mr May pleads for the Swedes, Dr Littledale strongly opposes their claims, and no Church historian of note ever sided with the Swedes. But through the American Church the Swedes can at any moment slip into the English Church; and where is *then* the Apostolical Succession of the English Church? My Orthodox brethren, beware! You might get into hot water.

When the Bishop of Gibraltar in his concluding speech in the last Conference was enlarging on his hearty reception by the Orthodox Bishops in the East, and that he was treated as a Brother Bishop, alluding to the validity of Anglican Orders, I could not help thinking to myself, that the Right Reverend gentleman should rather have first settled the more important question of the *Validity of Anglican Baptism.* I was therefore not a little astonished, when I saw a proof of this year's Report of the Anglo-Continental Society, and in it a curious piece of information, viz., the Bishop of Gibraltar asked the Patriarch of Constantinople, whether he would really have to re-baptize him, if he should join their Church? The Patriarch gave evasive answers, but the Bishop insisted on a clear answer, and the Patriarch returned an answer in the *affirmative!* Thus the dream of the Recognition of Anglican Orders by the Orthodox was most effectually dispelled. Or can the Ordination of a man be recognised, if his Baptism is *not* recognised?

As to the *Filioque*, on which both Conferences, but particularly the second treated, I must reserve this subject for another essay. Let us only append some straggling remarks, and survey our gains. Although the insertion of the *Filioque* into the Creed has been declared illegal, no thesis has been proposed requiring its removal. Yet this ought to have been the first step towards mending matters. It is clear that

Döllinger did not bring forward such a proposition, because
the Anglicans are tied by the law of their Establishment, and
utterly unable to accede to such a request. Thus, even if
the Anglicans held the Orthodox doctrine, but retained the
*Filioque*, all hope of union would be gone. *Let the Orthodox
not forget or overlook this!* We are more hopeful about the
Old Catholics, who promised to remove the *Filioque* from
their Creed and Catechism. This is, no doubt, a greater gain
for us, than if the Anglicans had assented, and the Old
Catholics dissented.

The six final theses on the procession of the Holy Ghost
are a SIGNAL VICTORY OF ORTHODOXY, although it must be
admitted, that in them much secondary matter encumbering
and obscuring the main subject has been introduced. Moreover we regret, that the theses were somewhat hurriedly proposed, and the voters, as it were, taken by surprise. The
consequence is, that the Anglicans, as far as we can judge,
have not understood them, or have withdrawn their assent.
Canon Liddon, *e.g.*, writes as follows to the *Spectator*,
respecting some statements which have been made about the
proceedings of the recent Conference at Bonn :—

" Pray forgive me for saying that you are under a strange
misapprehension when you state that ' the exclusion of the
*Filioque* from the Creed ' was ' granted by Dr Döllinger and
Canon Liddon ' at the recent Conference. What the Conference did may be stated as follows :—It admitted, as Bishop
Pearson has already admitted, that the *Filioque* had been
inserted in an Œcumenical Creed by an inadequate authority
and therefore irregularly. It formulated certain propositions
which might serve to show *that when the Latins accept and
the Easterns reject the Filioque they do not differ*, as has been
too generally supposed ; since the Latins reject any assertion
of two principles or causes in the Godhead, and the Easterns
admit a μεσιτεία of the Son in the eternal procession of the
Holy Spirit from the Father. Whatever may have been the
hopes or fears of individual members of the Conference, no
proposition was brought forward this year respecting the
exclusion of the *Filioque* from the Creed of the Western
Church. Speaking for myself, *I trust that no such proposi-*

*tion will be proposed hereafter.* For although the *Filioque* has never been affirmed by any Œcumenical Council, *it results by necessary inference from the language of Holy Scripture, and it expresses a revealed truth of the Divine nature.* To exclude it from the Western Creed would, I fear, do a great deal more than correct an ecclesiastical irregularity ; it would too probably create a popular impression that to attribute to the Son any part in the eternal procession of the Holy Ghost from the Father is not in accordance with God's revealed truth. Of instructions addressed by the Holy Synod to its delegates at the Conference we English heard nothing. If they were really given they would only have affected a minority of the representatives of the Eastern‑Church. And of the subjects which you mention I do not remember that any was discussed either in the committees or public meetings of the Conference—if we except the question raised parenthetically by Dr Overbeck about the Seventh Council. If these questions do emerge hereafter, I am sanguine enough to hope that they will be found to present less serious difficulties than you would appear to anticipate."

Meyrick in his address, delivered in Lincoln Cathedral (mentioned above), p. 5, says, "that some true doctrine is expressed by them" (*i.e.*, the words *Filioque*). And p. 6 : "The doctrine of the Double Procession in Eternity, properly expounded, *is a tenet of the Anglican Church.*" The Bishop of Gibraltar, in his final speech (Bericht, 1875, p. 113, *seq.*) said : "We have been assured, that those theses contain no new dogma, but that they are a patristic explanation of that dogma, *which has always been maintained by the Western Church.*" And p. 114 : "This morning it was said, the result of the labours of these divines had been the conviction, *that no essential difference exists between the views of the Eastern and Western Church with respect to the mysterious doctrine.*" Now I ask my Orthodox friends, how do these Anglican views agree with the end of the third thesis, which all of them have accepted : (Τὸ πνεῦμα τὸ ἅγιον) οὐκ ἐξ αὐτοῦ (*i.e.*, τοῦ Υἱοῦ) ἔχον τὴν ὕπαρξιν? Do these words not plainly exclude all co-operation of the Son in the existence of the Holy Ghost, or (as Liddon gives it) all μεσιτεία of the Son in the procession of the Holy Ghost? Thus with the Anglicans we have gained *absolutely nothing.* They stand exactly where they stood before the discussion. They prove in this point, as they have proved in other points, and as they will prove in the rest, *that if we will take them into our Union, as they are, without changing anything, we are welcome to do so.* And we must answer, *that if we did so, we should be traitors to Orthodoxy, and the most silly people into the bargain.* We admire Döllinger's acuteness, but do not envy his task merely to find out the best dress in which the Anglican doctrines may present themselves most attractively. Now as to the Old Catholics, have they sincerely and *ex animo* accepted the six theses? Of course, we do not know, but our presumption is in favour of them. We should simply like to ask them : "Do you, with respect to the procession, still believe the same as you did before the Conference?" Menzel in his Memorandum (Bericht, 1875, p. 135) has neatly and correctly expressed the Orthodox doctrine in No. 2. Does he still hold to No. 3 ?

Now, unpleasant as it may be, I must say a few words in reply to a fierce and most unjust attack on my character, and on the part I took in the last Bonn Conference. This attack was made in an article of the *Saturday Review* (August 21, 1875), eagerly reprinted in High Church papers. Here is the scrap, and my readers may judge whether it is a fair, honest, and gentlemanly dealing, or a bad imitation of a naughty street-boy, who from a safe hiding-place pelts dirt on the inoffensive passer-by. If the anonymous writer is a man of honour, let him come forward, show his face, and *retract his false statements.* The whole tenor of this insidious and sneering attack forcibly reminds me of the French saying : " *Vous avez tort, car vous vous fâchez.*" Here is the scrap : "The Conference was characterised by a few incidents which deserve a passing notice. The Anglicans were somewhat surprised to find Dr Overbeck seated among the Oriental divines. It may perhaps be necessary to explain that Dr Overbeck is a gentleman of whom the world first heard as a fervid Ultramontane priest. He then became a Lutheran, then an Anglican clergyman; and for the present he is a member of the Eastern Church. Through all his theological gyrations, however, he has been faithful to the ingrained bitterness of his Ultramontane training, and he has accordingly devoted his energies as an Orthodox Churchman to the task of vilifying the communions which he has abandoned. The first note of discord was introduced into the Conference by him, and it was only the mingled tact and firmness of Dr Döllinger and honest conciliatory temper of the Orientals which prevented a rupture. The following day Dr Overbeck was observed to take his seat no longer among the Oriental divines, but among the reporters. He had evidently received a hint." Now my reply.

As I have been these ten years a member of the Orthodox Church, and am a Doctor of Divinity, I had a perfect right to sit among the Oriental divines, so much the more, as most of them are my personal friends. It is perfectly indifferent to me, whether the Anglicans were surprised at it or not. Let them simply mind their own business.

I never was an Ultramontane, but always belonged to the Liberal school of thought.

I never joined the Anglican Church.

As to my " theological gyrations," I beg to quote Rückert's verses :

> " Das sind die Weisen,
> Die durch Irrthum zur Wahrheit reisen ;
> Die bei dem Irrthum verharren,
> Das sind die Narren."

If the article writer thinks, that a man who comes to a better understanding must, nevertheless, stick to his former wrong notions, and may not follow the dictates of his conscience, I cannot help him. Whoever is curious to know the history of my religious opinions, may read it in my book : " Die Orthodoxe Katholische Anschauung."

*I did not receive any hint* either from Döllinger, or from another Old Catholic, Anglican, or Orthodox, but did not occupy my former seat in front of Döllinger, *because* I felt insulted and disgusted at the treatment I had experienced. In the evening of the day, when the tumultuous scene took place, more than a dozen of my Orthodox friends expressed to me their sympathy, and declared their indignation at the proceedings. In the next meeting, Döllinger came to me and *explained* the matter to me, and we parted with a friendly shaking of hands. *I never should have wished to touch the matter again,* had not the Saturday Reviewer stirred it up, and by venomous intimations attacked my honour.

Now a word about "*vilifying.*" Many Anglicans are a particularly sensitive class of people. If you tell them an unpleasant truth in plain words, they call it *vilifying.* So, *e.g.*, if one says, your Church is heretical, *and proves it by stubborn facts,* they fly into a passion, resort to abusing, call him all sorts of names, impertinent, impudent, &c., as if all this rage amounted to the force of an argument. Why not sit down and refute the attack, and show that the facts are untrue? I should be only too glad. I wish the Anglicans were right, but how can you alter facts? If the facts speak against you, what is the use of shutting your eyes? You must either meet them and act accordingly, or betray the truth, and conform to circumstances. If then a smarting ray of light flashes across your eyes, or a shrill sound of truth makes you uncomfortable, do not accuse the light and the truth, but your own halting and undetermined self. And if a Churchman would say, I for one do not profess the heresies you refer to, would that alter the matter? No, you are a member of the Church, and a *bond of solidarity* binds you to the whole. If you are content to live in the same Church with low and broad Churchmen, you must take the guilt of their heresies also on your shoulders, or sever the unnatural bond. Here, my readers, you have a specimen of my *vilifying.* Now I have done with the *Saturday Review.*

Hitherto I have proposed my views respecting the Bonn Conferences, let us now hear some voices from the English Church. First, a loud voice from the *Ritualists.* If I am not mistaken, I have read somewhere in one of Meyrick's letters, that the Ritualists were only a handful of men who did not count. Now, let Mr Meyrick apply to the *Church Times* and *Church Review* for the number of Ritualistic churches in London, and he will be startled in the extreme. The article runs as follows :—" The decision of the Bonn Conference on the vital question of Anglican orders, and the consequent recognition of the Anglican Church as the Church of God in England, have entirely altered the position of the Catholic party, and changed the character of the contest in which it is engaged. For three hundred years and more the existence of the High Church school has been acknowledged and its influence felt, but it has always been an object of jealousy with politicians, and a thorn in the side of pretenders to spiritual authority. Regarded with cold indifference and *suspected of heresy by the Orientals,* treated as schismatical and apostate by the Papists, envied and hated by the Protestants, frowned upon and oppressed by successive generations of statesmen, it has had a hard struggle to maintain. The battle is now fought, and the victory won. Our true position is now known. The Anglican Communion is no sect, no creature of the civil power, no mere religious establishment, but an integral portion of the one Catholic and Apostolic Church. As such she must henceforward be recognised by all who, rejecting corrupt human inventions and baseless pretensions to new revelations, are content to hold to the faith once for all delivered to the saints, and *to take their stand on the firm foundation of the doctrines and practices of the undivided Church* [!?]. But, further (and this is the gist of the whole matter), the Catholic party *is the sole living representative* of those who have maintained these doctrines and these practices in times past. The other parties in the Church have, through the marvellous interposition of an overruling Providence, preserved the organic unity of the Church; but *this alone has adhered to the traditions of the primitive fathers,* maintained the integrity of the faith, and preserved the true idea of worship; this alone has clearly understood the *importance of sound dogmatic teaching,* upheld the authority, and laboured for the restoration of the corporate unity of the Church. This, then, is no party of strange views and rebellious tendencies, to be tolerated as long as necessary, and stamped out when convenient, but *the real heart and soul of the Anglican Church,* its connecting link with the past, its hope for the future. Take it away, and what will be left to the Establishment? Nothing but the tottering ruins and legal props of a once glorious fabric, the shattered remnants of a society that has proved itself unworthy of the sacred trust committed to it.

"Our past position was one of struggle for existence, our present is one of great honour and high privilege, but also of tremendous responsibility and urgent duty; our future will depend upon the manner in which those privileges are appreciated, the frankness with which those responsibilities are accepted, and the fidelity and zeal displayed in the discharge of those duties. What those responsibilities and duties are it is not difficult to perceive. Recent events have uttered no confused or unintelligible sound; present circumstances speak with no uncertain voice. Our task is twofold: first, one part of our work is at home—to *Catholicise our own portion of the Church.* Yes, we must neither hesitate to make the avowal, nor shrink from undertaking the work. We have to un-heathenise, un-Protestantise, and un-Romanise various sections of our own countrymen, then to Catholicise or evangelise them all. The second part of our work is abroad, and is to be instrumental in reuniting the now separated and hostile sections of Christendom into one corporate society—to lay hold of Romanism with the one hand, and of Protestantism with the other, and with our faces towards the East to lead them back into the old paths from which they have strayed, and thus *by the infusion of new blood to stir up the* WITHERED CORPSE OF ORTHODOX FORMALISM *into vigorous activity.* This is our vocation, we must not shrink from it. This is our mission, we dare not refuse to undertake it. It is no work of our own seeking, but a task assigned us, a duty imposed upon us. We have no choice. .

"Nor when we come to look carefully at all the circumstances, does it seem that this work ought after all to be one of very great difficulty. The chain of causation, directing our glance far back into the mists of mediævalism—the long course of events leading up to the present renewed life of the Church—plainly show that a grand design, of which the world has been oblivious, is being rapidly developed. The first beginnings of the Catholic revival are to be sought far back amidst the changes of the sixteenth century. The first foundations of the Oxford movement were laid during the Tudor dictatorship. *Cranmer, and Ridley, and their coadjutors, if rightly understood, would be recognised as the real predecessors of Newman, and Pusey, and their fellow-labourers.* This is so incontrovertible that it appears quite unnecessary to call for proofs. .

"In the sixteenth century an excellent design was spoiled, a glorious opportunity well-nigh lost. Once again, in the latter half of this nineteenth century, the opportunity presents itself, and under more favourable circumstances than before. Once more England's princes and her people, and especially Church people—bishops, priests, and laymen—are upon their trial before God. *The Ritualists are the salt to season the mass, the light to guide them into the right way.* They have but to stand firmly on the basis of the undivided Church [!?], to maintain steadfastly the primitive faith, to adhere strictly to the ancient usages, and to walk resolutely in the old paths, and their vocation will be accomplished, their mission fulfilled."

Now what do you say of this? Splendid rhetoric, brilliant words, electrifying effect! But do not look more closely, do not dissect the body of the phraseological texture, you would find little substance at the bottom. First of all, it was rather indiscreet and unwise to cry out and exult, as if your Church by help of the Bonn Conference was saved from perdition, as if now only you were entitled to claim the Catholic character of your Church, etc. And what was, after all, the Bonn Conference? Was it an Œcumenical Synod with binding decrees, or merely a friendly meeting of private gentlemen, where resolutions were carried, which every one might give up the next moment, if he altered his opinion? Now then, why make such a fuss? Who did recognise the Anglican Orders? Dr Döllinger and Bishop Reinkens, and perhaps a few more Old Catholics. The Orthodox could not recognise them, since they are accustomed not to give their opinion, before their Church has spoken out. Thus the pretended result is scarcely worth mentioning, and consequently the Catholicity of your Church is no more proved now than it was before the Conference. You are not only "*suspected of heresy by the Orientals,*" but made responsible

for all the undeniable heresies taught in your Church, because
you do not sever the bond of solidarity. But what do you
care for the opinion of a " WITHERED CORPSE," which you consider the Orthodox Church to be ? Indeed, a fine and delicate
compliment, flowing from the tender mercies of a so-called
sister Church, anxious to get united with her, a *mithered
corpse !* She will infuse new blood into this *withered corpse !*
What is the use of infusing new blood into a corpse, *i.e.*,
a dead body ? Or do you mean to render " inflexible Orthodoxy " more elastic and pliable by the infusion of Anglican
blood ? Or do you consider the Orthodox Church a sick
child, whose life you will save by administering *the bitter
draught* of unsound doctrine, while you moisten the rim of
the physic-glass with the *sweet liquor* of Orthodox phraseology,
in order to *delude* the poor patient, and make him *quickly
swallow it down ?*

> " Così all' egro fanciul porgiamo aspersi
>   Di soave licor gli orli del vaso :
>   Succhi amari ingannato intanto ei beve,
>   E dall' inganno suo vita riceve."

God forbid that we ever should suffer the infusion of
unsound blood ! Now, my Orthodox brethren, what would
you call a man abusing your Church as a *withered corpse ?*
I call him an impudent vilifier. " Cranmer and Ridley the
predecessors of Newman and Pusey ! " What does Dr
Littledale say to that ? Of course by proper preparation,
interpretation, explanation, you may change black into white.
We had already more than enough of these explanations
in the Bonn Conferences. Finally I wonder what " the
tottering ruins," *i.e.*, the Low and Broad Church will say,
that the Ritualists are " *the sole living representative, the
real heart and soul of the Anglican Church ?* But enough of
Ritualistic modesty.

One of the three parties of the Anglican Church was not
at all represented in the Bonn Conferences, viz., the *Broad
Church.* This important party extends from the throne
through the ranks of the educated classes to the simple
artisan. What Dean Stanley is at court, and with the upper

ten thousand, Canon Charles Kingsley was for the sons of
" muscular Christianity," for the hard-working classes, and
Professor Maurice attracted crowds of artisans, particularly
at the time when he was still preaching his popular sermons
in Vere Street. Who does not know how deeply attached
the many pupils of Professor Jowett are to their master ?
Dr Temple, Bishop of Exeter, represents the Broad Church
on the Episcopal bench. Let us then hear a voice from the
Broad Church. The *Times* (August 16, 1875) writes :
" Schemes for ' the re-unification of Christendom ' seem so
good that they usually disarm the spirit of criticism. Yet
they may *lead to mischief by raising false hopes*, and such,
we fear, will be the result of the Old Catholic Conference at
Bonn. We all lament, of course, the discords of Christianity.
We all regret that so much of its strength should be spent
in fierce sectarian strife, which lets loose or quickens the
most selfish and the least scrupulous passions of our nature.
We would all gladly bring Protestant and Catholic, Dissenter
and Churchman, Eastern and Western Christian, into a state
of agreement and peace. To most of us, it is true, such a
task may seem so far beyond the possibility of fulfilment that
we should as soon try to unite the nations as the Churches of
Europe ; but leisurely divines may be excused for more hopeful anticipations. The efforts of the Old Catholic Conference, however, invite more serious attention, because the
chief attempt *must be a failure*, and because the indirect
effects will sow discord instead of peace. The slightest
description of its elements will suffice to show that the
English people at least would do well to treat it with absolute distrust. It is made up, in the first place, of a few
German divines.    . They are aided by some English
clergymen who cannot bear to be called Protestants.    .
Some American divines of the same school give the discussions a Transatlantic emphasis. An Oriental haze is
added by some Greek Churchmen.    It would be difficult
to find a more scanty representation even of Catholic Christianity. Yet, slender as the gathering is, it is forced to
display an almost ludicrous caution in drawing up such
articles of faith as will command the assent of the whole

assembly. If Dr Döllinger were to frame a theological formula in the clear language of ordinary life, the notes of discord would instantly become so loud and fierce as to be a satire on the hopes of peace. Hence he must make the articles of union so vague that they may seem to mean anything or nothing, according to the temper of the recipient. Even when thus drawn they are usually too clear at first, and the meaning has to be scooped out of them by amendments. They produce something like agreement only when they become something like a blank. A few days of this edifying work will complete the *verbal pacification*, and then the Conference will dissolve into splinters of theological anarchy, amid a dense shower of mutual good wishes.

" *A few English divines have, indeed, gone to Bonn, but they no more represent the Church of England than Dr Döllinger represents the Church of Rome. The handful of clergymen who are playing at a Council speak in the name of nothing but themselves.* The movement has failed so signally that, as our Special Correspondent stated on Saturday, there are not 20,000 Old Catholics in the whole of Prussia, while there are eight million adherents of the Pope.

" So far, the Conference invites no sterner censure than that which is merited by an organised waste of time. But the truth is that in England it will do harm if it should do anything at all. *The Bishop of Winchester and Canon Liddon give mischievous counsel when they invite their countrymen to seek for ' the re unification of Christianity '* in the Old Catholic Conference at Bonn. If charity should begin at home, so should peace. The English friends of the Old Catholics will find ample room for their pacifying spirit in their own country. Our own Established Church is not specially famed for harmony of doctrine or of deed. *When we have been forced to pass a special Act of Parliament to prevent the clergy from defying the law, when one section of them is engaged in prose= cuting another, and when nothing keeps them in the same com= munion but the secular forces of the Establishment, there is surely a magnificent field for the exercise even of a genius for cnociliation.* Equally inviting are the discords of the Non- conformist bodies, for they represent a theological chaos. If

Dissenters do not fight against each other with so much virulence as the rival sections of the Establishment, they leave nothing to be desired in the way of animosity when she is the object of their attack. *Would it not be well for the Bishop of Lincoln, the Bishop of Winchester, and Canon Liddon to try whether they can frame some terms of peace between High Church, Low Church, and Broad Church, between Church and Dissent,* so that all these bodies might do their common work in a spirit which would not be an absolute satire on the Gospel of Peace? This question will read like the bitterest irony. Those eminent dignitaries may reply that they find themselves *more in unison with such theologians as Dr Döllinger than with many of their brethren* in the English Church, or with their Nonconformist fellow-countrymen. IF SO, IT IS WELL THAT SO IMPORTANT A FACT SHOULD BE MADE CLEAR TO THE PEOPLE OF ENGLAND, FOR IT MAY HAVE GRAVE PRACTICAL CON-SEQUENCES. But, whether religious conciliation be possible or not at home, it is desirable at least that nothing should be done to strengthen our present war of intolerance; and yet such promises to be the effect of coquetting with the Old Catholics. The divines who seek for Christian unity at Bonn are the very men who exasperate Dissenters by such insults as the denial of the term 'reverend' to Wesleyan ministers, and their less responsible followers will scarcely join Non-conformist clergymen in doing even the neutral work of religion. The more strenuously they look for such unity as that which is advocated by Dr Döllinger, the more will they tend to cast their Dissenting countrymen beyond the pale of Christian fellowship, and quicken sectarian hate. Everybody may notice the practical effects of this unhappy strife, and those are kind indeed who do not see that it may lead to political as well as to moral discords. Forty years ago there was no such hostility between Churchmen and Dis-senters. While stoutly fighting their battles at times, they half forgot their differences at others on the common ground of philanthropy, and they can both claim a share in a series of imperishable reforms. *It would be an evil day for this country if any large portion of the clergy were to be deluded into a pursuit of such a theological will-o'-the wisp as the Old*

*Catholic movement,* for they would only add to the religious discords at home, and they would find that on the Continent they could secure at best a phantom unity."

And the same leading paper writes (August 18): "A telegram has announced that the Conference has come to an agreement in all essential points respecting the Double Procession. We should have been surprised if such a difficulty had baffled a body which commands the infinite resources of *verbal vagueness. Everybody will agree with everybody else when all deliberately use words for the purpose of concealing what they mean.* Such a process is so certain to smooth down all the discords of the Church, that we wonder at the smallness of the gathering at Bonn. Cardinal Manning should have gone as well as Dean Howson, and Canon Liddon should have been accompanied by Mr Spurgeon. They are all 'Old Catholics' in their own sense of the phrase, and a consummate theological artist like Dr Döllinger could easily have covered their disagreements with twenty masterpieces of mystification to which all could have assented. But, then, Cardinal Manning would have come back to England to denounce the enemies of the Pope, and Mr Spurgeon to denounce the Pope himself, while Canon Liddon and Dean Howson would have felt as much bound as ever to teach contradictory versions of Christian theology. *When men differ from each other essentially, it is childish folly to try to unite them by an unmeaning phrase.* Dr Döllinger and his friends are playing at a ridiculous game of verbal jugglery. They agreed with each other at the end of the Conference just as little as they did at the beginning, and they know that their professions of harmony are idle talk."

And *Daily News* (August 18): "It may seem a little cruel to dash any of the high hopes with which the Conference closed, but the cool observer from a distance will assuredly be inclined to ask whether disputations and resolutions and votes on such subjects have usually been found in history to lead to a thorough unity of opinion among the various divisions of the Christian Church. So far as the proceedings of the Conference themselves have yet been reported, they seem to ordinary readers to suggest *rather a compromise of words than a cordial concurrence of sentiment.* The Church of Rome, indeed, can impose or impress on her own members something like a substantial unity. When the matters have been discussed long enough there is the authority at hand to pronounce a decision, and quiet souls within the Church trouble themselves no more about it. But the agreement which can thus be obtained and exhibited does not seem to be of much account in affecting the religious opinions of the rest of the world. It does not appear to the critical observer that the views at which the Conference at Bonn has arrived would gain much in their power to influence mankind even if they had an authority like that of Rome to proclaim them dogmas." And the *Hour:* " A telegram from Bonn brings the intimation of the close of the Conference of the friends of Christian Church Union. It was closed amid congratulations, as if a great work had been accomplished by the amount of agreement which had, after much discussion, been found to exist on certain knotty points of controversial theology. The Archbishop Lykurgos, of Syra, went so far as to express a belief that the issue of the proceedings would ultimately be the reunion of the divided Churches in one universal Church. We have every sympathy with the amiable idealists who indulge in these agreeable day-dreams. But when a body like the Old Catholics of Germany assume such an important function as Dr Döllinger claims for them, it is impossible to avoid scrutinising the reasonableness of the claim as well as the practicability of the purpose professed. Discussions on theological dogmas, we venture to say, have never yet reunited Churches or even individuals holding different views. How is it possible that such discussions as have taken place at Bonn can be the means of doing so? . . . . The whole idea of the Bonn Conference is a mistake. Dr Döllinger is a man whom to know is to revere, and who deserves the veneration of all the Churches; but he has lived in his study, and we need not wonder if he misconceives the real world, and pursues there the phantoms that delight him in his hours of studious meditation."

Let us now draw the conclusion. Can the Bonn Conferences lead to any satisfactory result, as long as they are carried on in the same spirit and in the same way as hitherto? No. Diplomatic manœuvres never were able to bring out the truth, but rather tended to obscure it. The most dangerous play is the *play at words,* so much the more dangerous and injuring, as our highest concerns are at stake. I for one prefer plain and straightforward dealing, and most decidedly decline idle logomachy.

But are then the Bonn Conferences to be discontinued? No, provided Döllinger can make up his mind *entirely to change his course of action.* The Anglicans are *not unitable,* as long as they are a state-bound and therefore *dogmatically irreformable Church.* It is a clear waste of time to transact with them, as you can at most attain to a more than doubtful *verbal* agreement. If Döllinger will devote his energies to make this truth palatable and acceptable to the Anglicans, we wish him God's speed, and will gladly assist him in such a good work. But if he attaches the Anglicans as a dead weight to our work of Reunion, *the sooner we withdraw the better.* The Union between the Orthodox and Old Catholics is an easy task, and we long for it, *but not on such ruinous conditions.* If you can for the moment not leave the Anglicans apart from your scheme of Union, your work will prove a hopeless trial.

The first step towards mending matters would be to induce Döllinger to state, in unmistakable terms, what he understands by " *the Church of Undivided Christendom,*" which he declares to be our common basis, but to which he never adhered. Shall it simply be an inviting sign-board without truth and reality? Let him properly define and accurately circumscribe this basis (in which, as a matter of course, the Seventh Œcumenical Synod must be included), and inviolably stick to it.

Let Döllinger remove the objectionable expression from his invitation, that after the Union the National Churches should be allowed to retain their " peculiarities in *doctrine.*" The Orthodox Church cannot allow a Church united with her to have *dogmas of her own.*

I know my antagonists will pounce upon me, will level

fiery darts at me, will lecture me with holy and unctuous indignation about irreverence, want of delicacy and personal consideration. Stop! such sermons are tedious, *produce facts and solid arguments*, and I will gladly answer you. If Döllinger is a public man, he must stand public criticism. Or should I, led by personal considerations, shut my mouth and refrain from warning my brethren, *as my conscience forcibly bids me?* I rather say with Newman: THE FIRST OF VIRTUES IS TO TELL THE TRUTH AND SHAME THE DEVIL.